EXTREME PLACES

Maria L. Lopes

Extreme Places

Coral reefs are the most dazzling and biologically diverse ecosystems in the world. They are also home to thousands of species of fish and other creatures.

Coral reefs can be found in the Indian and Pacific Oceans, the Caribbean Ocean, and the Red Sea. The Great Barrier Reef is the largest structure on Earth that is made by living creatures—so large it can be seen from outer space. Coral does not grow in cold water or close to where large rivers flow into the ocean.

Coral reefs are similar to underwater gardens. They are a paradise that doesn't have flowers but animals in the form of flowers. Where one coral dies, another one grows.

Coral reefs are diverse underwater ecosystems held together by calcium carbonate structures secreted by corals, colonies of tiny animals found in marine waters that contain few nutrients. Most coral reefs are built from stony corals, which consist of polyps that cluster in groups and grow in warm, shallow water.

They can take years to grow, some as long as 10,000 years. Coral reefs are the largest structures of biological origin on Earth, and they rival old-growth forests in the longevity of their ecological communities.

Coral and other reef inhabitants could potentially provide important medicines, including anti-cancer drugs, painkillers and anti-inflammatory compounds.

DID YOU KNOW?
Coral reefs take up to 10.000 years to grow!

The French remove angelfish is a grazer on the reef. Its nipper-like jaws enable it to deftly algae from the reef.

Parrotfish bite off chunks of coral with their heavy jaws. They expel the sand and digest whatever organic material is present. They sleep in a protected area of the reef surrounded by a mucous sheet that they secrete.

The peacock flounder usually lies on its side. Either on the surface with its mottled skin or hidden beneath a layer of sand, it is quite difficult to spot.

Moray eels, including the spotted moray eel, are common reef inhabitants; their unique body forms enable them to fit into cracks and crevices in the reef. Safe from predation themselves, they can wait to prey on other animals.

Clownfish are from the Indian-Pacific region. They work their way into an anemone gradually, allowing the anemone to get used to the fish and not trigger the anemone's stinging response.

The yellowtail snapper is a common reef fish. The black stripes on its head both hide the eyes and serve to disorient predators attacking schools of this gregarious fish.

When coral reefs are stressed by changes in temperature, light, or nutrients, they expel the symbiotic algae living in their tissues and become white. When this happens, the coral is not dead, but rather under stress, and therefore, more vulnerable. Coral bleaching is an issue today as our climate changes and temperatures rise.

However, in a recent study, it was found that sponges can keep a reef alive by recycling vast amounts of organic matter to feed snails, crabs, and other creatures. So sponges are one hope for the continued survival of coral reefs. They recycle nearly ten times as much matter as bacteria, and produce as much nutrition as all the corals and algae in the reef combined.

SHARKS

(DID YOU KNOW?
Sharks can live up
to 70 years!)

Sharks have lived in the oceans since dinosaurs walked the earth. There are more than 400 species of shark and they can live into their 70s—three times longer than what was originally thought. A shark's daily routine starts at the bottom of the ocean. They work their way up to the surface as a pack, swimming in fast circles until sunset. After dark, they separate and hunt alone.

Great white sharks are born to kill. When chasing prey, their entire body can leap out of the water. Great whites have no table manners, but they do have serrated teeth that a steak knife would envy.

The silver tip shark is much more fearsome than the great white shark, with a swimming speed of approximately 72 kilometres per hour. It gobbles down anything it can catch, including barracuda and other sharks in the open sea.

Barracuda

Another large hunter is the barracuda. The barracuda is a super hunter and a monster munching machine. The warm water in the coral reef makes a perfect home for the barracuda. They have a fierce reputation because they generate a sudden burst of speed to catch their prey by surprise. They attack almost anything, even if they eat only a little of it.

Whales live in groups called a pod. The Narwhal lives in the Arctic Ocean. They have a single spiral tusk. This tusk is a long tooth, and they use it to defend themselves. They are not aggressive though, and rub their tusks together to communicate with each other. Their long tooth or tusk makes them akin to aquatic unicorns.

The Beluga whale is another creature that lives in the Arctic waters. They travel from one area to another throughout the narrow channels or cracks in the ice. Adult belugas are pure white. They are very noisy—cheeping and chirruping, and sometimes they chime like a bell when talking to each other. Their voice range also includes sounds similar to whistles and squeaks.

Blue whales spend the summer in cold waters, where there is plenty of food. They migrate to warmer, shallow water when the females give birth.

Humpback whales visit polar water only to feed. The ice often extends far over the water, and during the winter, these whales can became trapped and die if their breathing hole in the ice closes up.

The orcas that visit the polar water often hunt together. They attack seals or penguins on the small ice floes; one orca tips over the ice while the others wait to catch the prey. The Orcas also hunt and eat the Beluga and the Narwhal. In some areas, they are devastating the populations of both.

WHALES

DID YOU KNOW?

The Blue Whale is the biggest creature in the world. It is as long as a Boeing 737, and weighs more than twenty elephants!

SEA BIRDS

DID YOU KNOW?

Birds developed from reptiles! The albatross has a wingspan as wide as an elephants is tall!

Sea birds are great divers. They do a great amount of their feeding under water. When the water puffin dives under water, it becomes hard to swim. Some sea birds, such as gulls, keep close to whales because whales drive fish and krill to the surface of the water- a fishy banquet for the gulls.

Albatross also live and feed on what is in the sea, and storms do not stop their hunting. Their long slender wings are perfectly shaped for catching the wind and gliding. The albatross swoops down to the surface of the water and catches slippery fish and squid in its large bill. They cover huge distances, as much as 1,000 kilometres in just one day.

Arctic terns have a very extreme lifestyle. They build their nests in the Arctic during the summer. When their young have fledged and become independent, they then fly to Antarctica. There they winter during the Antarctic summer, before flying back again to the Arctic to breed the following year. They take advantage of food at the peak of the season and avoid food shortages.

Life on the Ice and Tundra

Adélie penguins spend half their lives on the sea ice that surrounds the Antarctic, diving into the icy water to find food for their chicks.

They are great swimmers, but clumsy on land.

They can't fly, so the water is their home. They use their wings as flippers, and three layers of short feathers keep out the cold.

They swim by using their tail to steer and their feet to paddle.

DID YOU KNOW?
In emergencies, male emperor penguins can produce milk to feed chicks!

DID YOU KNOW?

The liver of the polar bear is poisonous! A polar bear sometimes goes green, when algae gets inside its hollow hairs!

POLAR BEAR

The polar bear is the largest and most powerful predator in the Arctic. To survive, the polar bear spends half his life searching for food. Polar bears can swim long distances, and they can stay in the ice water for more than one hour. Polar Bear are mammals and have a thick layer of fat to keep them warm. In the water, they use their front paws as paddles and steer with their hind legs.

Their excellent senses help them find prey either on or under the ice. They usually hunt ringed seals by waiting for the seals near their breathing holes in the ice called "aglus" and then pouncing. The polar bear needs an average of 2 kilograms (kg) (4.4 pounds [lbs.]) of food per day to obtain enough energy to survive. A ringed seal weighing 55 kg (121 lbs.) could provide up to eight days of energy for a polar bear. They are opportunistic hunters, always on the alert for a kill. Belugas whales and young walruses are on their menu, as well as, berries and seaweed in the warmer months. Polar bear cubs are born in November through January in a den. Mother and cubs come out in late spring. Mother bears look after their cubs for as long as 30 months.

Due to global warming, the ice floes that polar bears once relied on to take them out hunting into the open ocean are disappearing fast. These days, many polar bears starve to death in summer, or take up residence close to small Hudson Bay towns, raiding rubbish dumps and causing problems. There are still enough ice floes for spring and winter hunting, but who knows what the future will bring.

Another animal from the remote Arctic is the walrus. Mature males grow tusks as symbols of power and hunt for food on the bottom of the ocean. They are clumsy on land and ice, and they spend two thirds of their life under the water. They can also sleep under water, using a sack in their throat that they fill with air.

Other animals

Arctic foxes live in areas where the tundra turns to shrubs and trees. They are small animals, sized 3 to 8 kg (6.5 to 17 lbs.) and 75 to 110 centimetres (cm) long (2.3 to 3.5 feet), including their tail. The females are slightly smaller than the males.

Their ears point forward, giving them keen directional hearing. They can hear small animals moving through tunnels beneath the snow. This excellent hearing allows the Arctic fox to pounce and dig down for a quick meal of rodents, without the need to see their meal beforehand.

DID YOU KNOW?
Walruses gets its name from a Swedish word meaning 'Whale horse'!

DID YOU KNOW?
Polar wolfs hunt in pack to take down large animals!

The polar wolf, or white wolf, is an animal of the far North. It lives its whole life above the Northern tree line in the Arctic tundra. These wolves survive in some of the coldest places on earth.

They have anatomical, behavioural, and physiological adaptations that allow them to survive in this hostile environment, including smaller ears to prevent heat loss and thick layers of fur. The inner layer of fur is shorter and softer for extra insulation.

These wolves hunt in packs to take down large animals such as caribou and musk oxen. They also catch smaller prey individually, such as hares and lemmings.

Musk oxen are found in the treeless areas of the Arctic. They were reintroduced to other areas around the Arctic during the 20th century, because they had died out from being hunted into extinction. They are grazing animals, more closely related to sheep and goats than to oxen.

Their Latin name, "Ovibos," means "sheep-ox." They have a long shaggy coat, which gives them the appearance of being larger and more powerfully built than they really are.

Some of their hairs can be as long as 60 cm (24 inches). Musk oxen feed on grasses and seasonal wild flowers in the spring and summer months, which they often spend in river valleys near water.

DID YOU KNOW?

Many lemmings drown when they migrate, but the belief that they commit suicide by leaping off cliffs is not true!

Lemmings are small rodents that can be found near the Arctic, in tundra biomes. They have long, soft fur and a long tail. They are herbivorous, feeding on leaves, roots, grasses, sedges, and bulbs. They do not hibernate, but remain active through the harsh Northern winter. They find food by burrowing through the snow and using grasses chipped and stored in advance.

Other small animals

Snowshoe hares are a bit larger than the typical rabbit. They have taller hind legs and longer ears. They have a snow-white winter coat that turns brown in the spring. They feed at night, in the forest, on grasses, shrubs, and other plants.

Plant life in the Arctic is characterized largely by what grows on the tundra, a vast low growing treeless area of approximately 11.5 million square kilometres that is mainly underlain with permafrost.

There are low shrubs as tall as 2 metres (7 feet), and in rare places, sedges, grasses, mosses, and liverworts, as well as, an extensive variety of alpine flowering plants and lichens. In all, there are about 1,700 species of plants that live on the tundra.

The tundra can support many larger herbivores including reindeer, musk oxen, lemmings, arctic hares, and squirrels. To the southern edge of the Arctic, the tundra can cover around 80% to 100%. Yet farther north, the percentage can drop to around 0%, with just a few hardy alpine plants growing in sheltered microclimates.

GLOSSARY

Algae	Simple water plants with no true stems or leaves
Caribou	A North American reindeer
Den	A wild animal's lair
Herbivore	An animal that feeds only on plants
Lichen	A low-growing dry plant that grows on rocks
Liverwort	A green plant that grows on the surface of rocks. They are usually associated with compacted soil or poor drainage. Although they don't harm other plants, they inhibit the growth of small or young plants.
Mammal	An animal that produces milk
Microclimate	A local atmospheric zone where the climate differs from the surrounding area. The term may refer to areas as small as a few square feet (for example, a garden bed), or as large as many square miles.
Moss	A small green plant that grows in damp places
Plankton	Tiny plants and animals that are found floating close to the surface of ponds, lakes and seas. Plankton are at the bottom of the ocean food chain. They are called "producers" because they make their own food using sunlight
Pod	A group of whales or dolphins
Scavenger	An animal that feeds on the bodies of dead animals
Sea Ice	Ice that forms on the ocean surface as sea water freezes
Tundra	A vast, flat, Arctic region where the subsoil is permanently frozen

http://www.ecokids.ca/pub/eco_info/topics/oceans/coral_reefs.cfm

Meet South American River Monsters. Have you ever seen them? You haven't? Then take a look inside this book...

When Oliver spent the day at the beach with his grandfather, he didn't expect an old sailing ship to take him on a wild adventure.

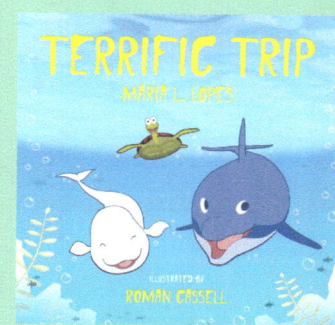

Eddie and Bella, embark on an unexpected adventure, to be reunited with their friend, the white beluga, in the North Pole.

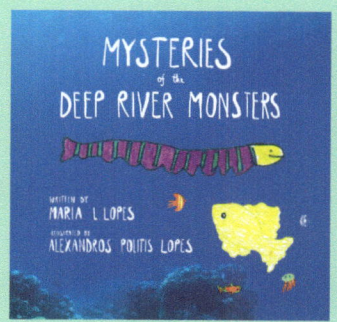

Amazon, this great river, does not give away its secrets easily. In the dark water, there are hidden dangers. Come, explore it!

In Boogie Woogie Woo we meet a young boy and his pet mouse who love to perform their favourite songs by tapping and singing.

Rainforest Animals brings readers up close with rainforest animals that are in danger of extinction because of the loss of habitat.

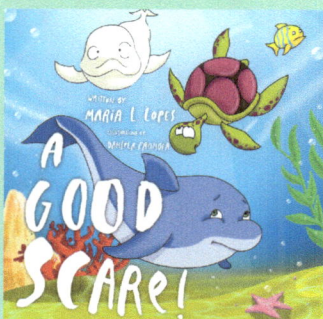

In A Good Scare we meet a young beluga whale, Tina, who is separated from her pod and swims far way from her northern home.

This book is aimed at very young children. The bright colours and pictures are designed to develop language awareness.

EXPLORE ONE OF THE MOST FASCINATING HABITATS ON EARTH.

From the great barrier reef in the Indian and Pacific Oceans, to the frozen landscapes Arctic and Antarctic are home to many fascinating creatures.